RAINBOW VISION

JOURNAL

ORANGE

How to have awesome experiences without worrying about time or money

SHARON DAWN

Published by: Rainbow Vision Journal
                  PO Box 1062, Airlie Beach, Qld, Australia 4802
                  www.rainbowvisionjournal.com
                  Email: smile@rainbowvisionjournal.com

Cover Design by: Sharon Dawn
Illustrations by: Sharon Dawn
Typeset by: Adam Press

ISBN Hardcover: 978-0-6487662-3-0
ISBN Paperback: 978-0-6487662-4-7
ISBN eBook: 978-0-6487662-5-4

 A catalogue record for this work is available from the National Library of Australia

The information given in this journal should not be used as a substitute for professional medical advice. Any use of the information in this journal is at the reader's discretion and risk. Readers who are experiencing adverse effects from any situation arising from using this journal should seek professional counselling. Neither the author nor the publisher can be held responsible for any loss, claim or damage arising from use, or misuse, of the suggestions made in this journal.

DEDICATION

I dedicate this journal to everyone who chooses to experience life in the best way possible.

CONTENTS

WHAT IS RAINBOW VISION JOURNAL   vii

FREE GIFTS   ix

HOW TO USE THIS JOURNAL   1

     I am Silent and Listen   7

     Catching My Chaser Thoughts   9

     Finding My Gold Nuggets   11

     I am so Grateful for   13

FILL MY BUCKET   15

     My Perfect Home   16

     Skills to Learn   18

     Create Awesome Experiences   20

     Places to Visit   22

     My Favourite Style of Holiday   24

     Things to Own   26

     Something Else   28

     Journal Time   32

FINDING THE GEMS   35

     What is My Number One?   37

     Dream Catcher Jar   39

     Connecting My Dreams   41

         My Perfect Home   42

         Skills to Learn   44

         Create Awesome Experiences   46

         Places to Visit   48

         My Favourite Style of Holiday   50

         Things to Own   52

         Something Else   54

     Journal Time   56

LET'S GET CREATIVE

	61
Orange Words	62
Orange Thoughts	63
My Perfect Home	64
Skills to Learn	66
Create Awesome Experiences	68
Places to Visit	70
My Favourite Style of Holiday	72
Things to Own	74
Something Else	76

BRING IT ALL TOGETHER

	79
Manifesting Exercise	81
My Perfect Home - Story	82
Skills to Learn - Story	86
Create Awesome Experiences - Story	90
Places to Visit - Story	94
My Favourite Style of Holiday - Story	98
Things to Own - Story	102
Something Else – Story	106
It's Magic	111
Revising my Chaser Thoughts	115
The Magic Rewritten	119
3 Action Steps	125
My Reward	127
Check In	129
Journal Time – Keep up the Magic	130
What's Next?	135
Draw like a Child	136
Write from Within	137
Congratulations	181

RED — My Heart

How to follow your heart and find your bliss without reliving your past.

ORANGE — My Experiences

How to have awesome experiences without worrying about time or money.

YELLOW — My Well-being

How to feel good regardless of your body shape or fitness level.

GREEN — My Abundance

How to attract money and abundance into your life without the stress.

BLUE — My Purpose

How to discover your true purpose regardless of your location and skill.

INDIGO — My Awareness

How to stay in control of your thoughts regardless of your situation.

VIOLET — My Connection

How to feel connected and thankful regardless of your faith or religion.

 GOLD — My Uniqueness

How to bring your life into alignment using your Rainbow Vision Steps.

What is the
RAINBOW VISION
JOURNAL?

The Rainbow Vision Journal is a series of eight guided workbooks that take you on a journey to discover your true self and your inner purpose.

Rainbow

Signifies new beginnings as you break through your current path, just as the sun breaks through the clouds after rain. The bridge symbolises your journey, leading you to your pot of gold.

Rainbows are a magical light that make us feel peaceful. They raise our energy vibration while reminding us that life is not always as we see it.

Vision

You have the ability to imagine, to create images and to plan your future. With vision you can look within, to see your true wisdom.

Journal

A safe place where you can capture your thoughts and ideas, plan your future, and release your past. A place where you can be honest with yourself. A place where you can be creative and be your true self.

Acknowledgements

I would like to thank all the people who have supported me in my desire to live my live on my terms.

I would also like to thank all the creative and inspirational people in the world. You continue to inspire us and enhance our journey.

FREE GIFTS

As a thank you for purchasing this journal please accept the following gifts. They are to inspire you on your journey.

- Download a guided meditation to do prior to journaling. This is a quick meditation that takes you into your heart.

  Go to *www.rainbowvisionjournal.com/meditation*

- Receive regular Rainbow Vision Journal eNewsletters for support and clarity on the topics discussed in this journal. All promotions and specials will be released via the eNewsletter prior to release on the website and Social Media. To Register, go to *www.rainbowvisionjournal.com* and click on 'Subscribe to eNewsletter.'

- Download the Rainbow Vision Journal FREE eBook.

  This eBook explains the concepts behind Rainbow Vision Journal including your inner child, energy vibration and the law of attraction. It discusses how the key to a great life is to be aware of our thoughts and feelings so we can align them to our heart's desire.

  www.rainbowvisionjournal.com

- Join us on Facebook and Instagram and become a member of the private Facebook group. Enjoy daily journal prompts and other interesting ideas as part of your ongoing journey into self-awareness and inner connection.

  Sharon Dawn and Rainbow Vision Journal

  @rainbow_vision_journal

- The GOLD journal will be made available for free to all readers who purchase the other seven. Conditions apply so keep your receipts.

When I go for a walk with no destination in mind, I will have a different experience than when I have chosen my path.

HOW TO USE
THIS JOURNAL

Life is to be enjoyed and experienced to its fullest. To be lived! Yet too often we find we are living on auto pilot, doing the same thing every week as we let our dreams slip away. We become concerned about what others think. We become afraid of failing. We worry about how silly our dreams are or how we could not possibly make them happen and so we let our dreams go. We allow our day to day life to unfold without much thought and then we wonder why life is not as exciting or fulfilling as we would like it to be.

It is the most natural thing in the world to want good things in our life, yet we have been taught that it is selfish to put ourselves first. I do not believe that it is selfish, in fact, I believe it is the most selfless thing we can do. When we are living our life the way we want, by following our dreams, we are filled with love and happiness. To be happy is the kindest gift we can give ourselves, our family and our friends. Just imagine our world full of happy people!

It's normal for us to desire nice things

I do not mean we should just go out and buy stuff! Buying things doesn't make us happy. It can give us a happy burst, a bit like an adrenalin burst, but it doesn't last because it is not true happiness. This type of buying can even lead us into an unhappy state because it is not filling our need like we hoped it would.

True happiness comes from knowing why we want certain things. When we know why something is important to us, we then buy for a whole different reason, and that reason is where we find our happiness. The goal of this journal is to discover what experiences would be awesome specifically for you. What dreams will make you really happy.

Commit to the vision of what you desire in your life.

Journaling connects us to our inner self. It helps us find clarity in what we want to experience, and it allows us to explore ideas that we might not want to share with others. In this journal, you have the opportunity to get clear on what experiences will make you happy.

Do you remember daydreaming and playing make-believe when you were a child? What did you want to do when you grew up? What about now? What are the things you have put off for years or said you will do one day? What would you do if you didn't think about time, money, or what others think?

Find time to dream

It could be designing your perfect home or travelling overseas in five-star luxury or in an RV. Maybe you would like to join a retreat somewhere exotic or swim with dolphins. Perhaps you would love to learn a new language, play a musical instrument, learn how to paint, learn how to use a computer better, take photos of sunsets around the world or write your own novel or story. Maybe you want to help your community, be with animals or sing on stage.

Imagine that you can have anything you want, that there are no limits. Ask what would my life be like? What would I be doing? You will be amazed how your heart opens to your true self when you ask yourself these questions and let yourself dream. It will uncover what is buried deep, almost forgotten, but not quite.

I believe in my dreams

We all have dreams so let your imagination run wild as you include everything that excites or inspires you, big or small. This is your bucket list on steroids!

Before you start your dreams lists, look through the journal to familiarise yourself with how it works. The left-hand pages are to capture any ideas that can help clarify your inner self. Write, scribble, draw or paste pictures. Do anything that inspires you. Anything that makes you smile or lets you play.

The next few pages in this first section are designed for you to use throughout the journal. I encourage you to go back to them often as you become aware of new things about yourself.

The first page is 'I am Silent and Listen.' It is to encourage you to set aside times to be silent and let your inner child guide you. Make a commitment to start listening from within. This is where your true happiness is, with regular practice it becomes easier for you to trust in it.

Be a deliberate creator of your life

Next is a page called 'Catching My Chaser Thoughts.' This is where you write any thoughts that are disempowering to you. Sometimes when we dream big, we immediately have chaser thoughts like "I cannot afford to do that"; "I do not have time for that"; or worse, "I cannot do that, people will laugh at me, people will think I am crazy!" As you build your lists, capture any resistance here. Write exactly what pops into your head, without analyzing it and near the end of the journal you will have the opportunity to revise these.

It's time to put the fun and excitement back into my life

'Finding My Gold Nuggets' is for you to capture any 'aha' moments. Anything that seems perfect to you that you don't want to forget. These help you write your magic at the end of this journal and become part of your pot of gold at the end of the rainbow.

The last page in this section is our gratitude page, where you remind yourself of all the wonderful things that you have. Making it a daily practice to be thankful elevates your energy vibration and is a great way to start your journal practice each day.

The second section in this journal is 'Fill my Bucket.' There are seven categories for you to build lists. Each is designed to help you think up everything you would like to experience. Capture the ideas that put a smile on your face and expand on the ideas that really excite you.

Try and come up with as many ideas as possible for each category and remember you can keep adding to them as more ideas come to you. Explore what you feel guided to experience. You may come up with ideas that scare you, so take the time to look at why it scares you. Maybe the idea is challenging you. The thought of jumping out of an aeroplane is very scary to many people, but under the fear, is there a true desire? Fear is something we have to protect us, but sometimes it gets in our way and stops us doing what we genuinely want. So, ask yourself, 'even though I am afraid, do I still want to experience this?'

If I can envisage it, I can do it

Once you have your lists, you will be guided to find connections between your ideas. You will dig deeper to gain further clarity on what you genuinely want each experience to be and how important each one is to you. Once you are clear on your lists, you will enjoy creating some visual concepts, then write your stories. You will bring it all together as you revise your chaser thoughts, write your magic story, and continue journaling.

Before starting your journal, put yourself into a happy space. Use one of your wonderful memories from your RED journal or think of something that makes your heart sing. Then ask for your inner child to show you your dreams.

If you need help to connect, download my RED meditation to connect to your heart.

www.rainbowvisionjournal.com/meditation

To get the most out of this journal, aim to complete only a few pages at a time. Don't rush it. Think deeply about each list and each question and see what comes to you, then journal further on your thoughts. Each page is designed to open your awareness so let your feelings guide you.

Two big things happen as you work through this journal. One, you get excited about your dreams again. Daydreaming is fun, its creative, and best of all, it helps you find your inner happiness. The second thing that happens is that we all attract what we think, so the more excited and happier you feel about something, the more you will attract that into your life.

A big dream takes no more effort than a small dream

Do not concern yourself on HOW you can afford your dreams or WHEN you will have the time to do all these things. Think ONLY about WHAT your dream is, what it truly looks and feels like, and the experience you desire. The clearer you are, the more likely you are to receive it.

So, your goal for this journal is to get really clear on the experiences you want, what really makes you happy within, and then have fun as you create your vision and start to bring your daydreams alive.

Keep asking

'Am I following my heart? Does this make me happy?'

THOUGHTS

Write or draw your thoughts

I am Silent and Listen

When you stop and let your mind be still, even for a moment, you open a space that allows your inner child's voice to be heard.

To quieten your mind and bring it to stillness, simply take 3 deep breaths in and out. Focus on your breath and let your mind fall into a space that has no thoughts. When a thought floats in, observe it, then let it go as you bring your focus back to the breath.

FIND MOMENTS TO BE PRESENT

I can be silent and in the moment when I brush my teeth, have a shower, make the bed, or even as I am waiting for the jug to boil.

....

....

....

....

....

....

....

....

....

Download your free meditation www.rainbowvisionjournal.com/meditation

THOUGHTS

Write or draw your thoughts

Catching My Chaser Thoughts

As you work through each exercise, negative thoughts may pop into your head. What are you saying to yourself when you are not paying attention? Write whatever comes into your mind.

Do not analyse or change it, simply capture it here.

E.g. I can't do this, I'm no good at daydreaming or writing

*When you are aware of your self-talk,
you can change whatever thoughts do not serve you*

THOUGHTS

Write or draw your thoughts

Finding My Gold Nuggets

Capture any inspiring thoughts, words, sayings, memories or 'aha' moments that motivate or inspire you.

This makes up part of your pot of gold at the end of the rainbow.

- ....
- ....
- ....
- ....
- ....
- ....
- ....
- ....
- ....
- ....
- ....
- ....
- ....
- ....
- ....

I consciously choose to follow my dreams

THOUGHTS

Write or draw your thoughts

I am so Grateful for

Create a daily practice giving thanks for the things you already have, like the air you breath, the sun on your face, the ground you walk on, the food you eat, the eyes you see through, the nose you smell with. We have so much we take for granted each day. Being grateful allows you to see how truly blessed you already are in this moment.

WE ATTRACT WHAT WE FOCUS ON

Thank You, Thank You, Thank You

Start your vision from a place of gratitude
to manifest what you are seeking.

FILL MY BUCKET

It's time to dream as BIG as you can. Do you have a dream list or bucket list? What are all the things you have told yourself you would love to do if only you had the time or money?

This section has seven categories to help you organise your thoughts. You may find you put one idea into a couple of categories.

1. My Perfect Home
2. Skills to Learn
3. Create Awesome Experiences
4. Places to Visit
5. My Favourite Style of Holiday
6. Things to Own
7. Something Else

Write down whatever comes to mind, no matter how silly it might seem. Write without analysing, just let your imagination run wild. It doesn't matter if you double up ideas across the categories as this shows what is strong for you. Grab your RED journal and include all the things you love as this will also help you gain clarity.

Think how each dream looks and feels. Do you want to dance the Salsa in Cuba, hot air balloon over the Victoria Falls, or learn to paint in Tuscany? Include everything you dream to do, everything you said you would do 'one day,' and everything that you are doing now that you love and want to continue doing.

OK, it's Playtime!

My Perfect Home

Write everything you can think of for your perfect home.
Where it is? What size, how many rooms, what colour? What features
does it have? What is the outlook from inside? What is special about it?
Look through magazines, go to display homes. Find what appeals to you.

Skills to Learn

Do you want to learn a new language, how to draw, paint, swim, sing? Perhaps you are in business or want to be in business and would like to learn leadership, marketing, IT or communication? Maybe you are a writer and want to complete a novel and self-publish it.

Create Awesome Experiences

What things have you said you would like to try one day? Maybe you want to paint in Tuscany, cook in Italy, snorkel the Great Barrier Reef, climb a Mountain or run a marathon? Maybe you want to sing in a musical, live in a different country or be involved in a certain charity.

Places to Visit

Where do you want to go? What do you want to see? What do you want to experience when you get there? Do you want to explore a certain city or country? Do you want to go around the world or go back to the same place every year? List all your ideas for holiday destinations.

My Favourite Style of Holiday

How do you like to travel? Do you like to stay in one place or drive around in a car or mobile home? Perhaps you prefer to cruise on a ship or fly and stay at 5-star accommodation. Maybe it is house swapping or free camping. Include how long you like to be away – weeks, months?

Things to Own

We all desire nice things. What specific things do you want to own?
Is it a certain type of car, mobile home or boat? Perhaps it is new
furniture, a specific painting, or a wardrobe full of shoes. Maybe
you are a collector and would love to expand that collection.

Something Else

Add anything that makes your heart sing that isn't on your other lists. It may be a hobby where you enjoy spending time, like sewing quilts, doing puzzles or selling handmade items at the markets. It could be playing tennis, going for walks, doing yoga or meditation classes.

Extra Pages

Journal Time

FINDING THE GEMS

Now that you have a good idea of all the things you would like to experience, it is time to rate them. Go back over your lists and put numbers in the left column showing the importance to you, one being most important. Do not think about when you can do these things or how you will pay for them, simply rate how important they are to you.

Next, grab a selection of coloured pens or pencils and circle the items that look like they may connect with each other. Find as many connections as you can to help you building your dream lists. You will then select your top seven dreams and start adding as many connections to them as seems right for you.

E.g. Say your number one place to visit is Japan. One of the experiences you want is to ski. One of the things you would love to see is Cherry Blossoms in full bloom and another is to stay in a traditional home in whichever country you are in. Maybe you want to learn a new language or just a few words. Perhaps you want to learn to write or take better photos and a holiday would be an opportunity for you to practice those skills. You may want to learn how to use social media better so this can also be connected to your trip. Circle the style of travel you prefer; the time frame you prefer to be away and any other experiences that may fit that destination.

Make connections with everything that fits together. Some may suit many experiences.

What is My Number One?

Usually our number one idea is easy to spot, so write that below for each category. However, it may not be so clear. If so, look to see if it becomes clearer when connected to other experiences. Try the dream jar idea on the next page or do a meditation connecting to your heart, asking your inner child for guidance. Journal each idea to gain further clarity.

You may want to change the titles below to suit your dreams.

My Perfect Home ....

....

Skills to Learn ....

....

Create Awesome Experiences ....

....

My Favourite Style of Holiday ....

....

Things to Own ....

....

Something Else ....

....

Download meditation https://www.rainbowvisionjournal.com/meditation

THOUGHTS

Write or draw your thoughts

Dream Catcher Jar

If you can't decide on which dreams are the most important to you then try this fun activity and create a dream jar.

- Find yourself a nice jar as it is important to feel excited when you look at your jar.

- Cut up a piece of paper into similar sized pieces, say 3cm by 10cm

- Write out each of the items you want on a separate piece of paper.

- Fold each one and think about it as you do, then put it in the jar.

- When you have finished, give the jar a good shake

- Close your eyes and connect within. Ask for guidance to choose the best idea for you at this time. See if you already have the feeling of which one you want or don't want to pull out first.

- If not, open the jar and pull out the one that feels right. If you dither and feel unsure, stop and redo the last step.

- Read the idea on the paper. How do you feel? Are you excited or relieved? Maybe you feel scared at what you have chosen. Take time to think about the emotions that have arisen. If you have chaser thoughts put them on your chaser page as these are clues to what is holding you back.

You can also use your dream catcher jar by placing each of your dreams in the jar and place it where it makes you smile each time you see it.

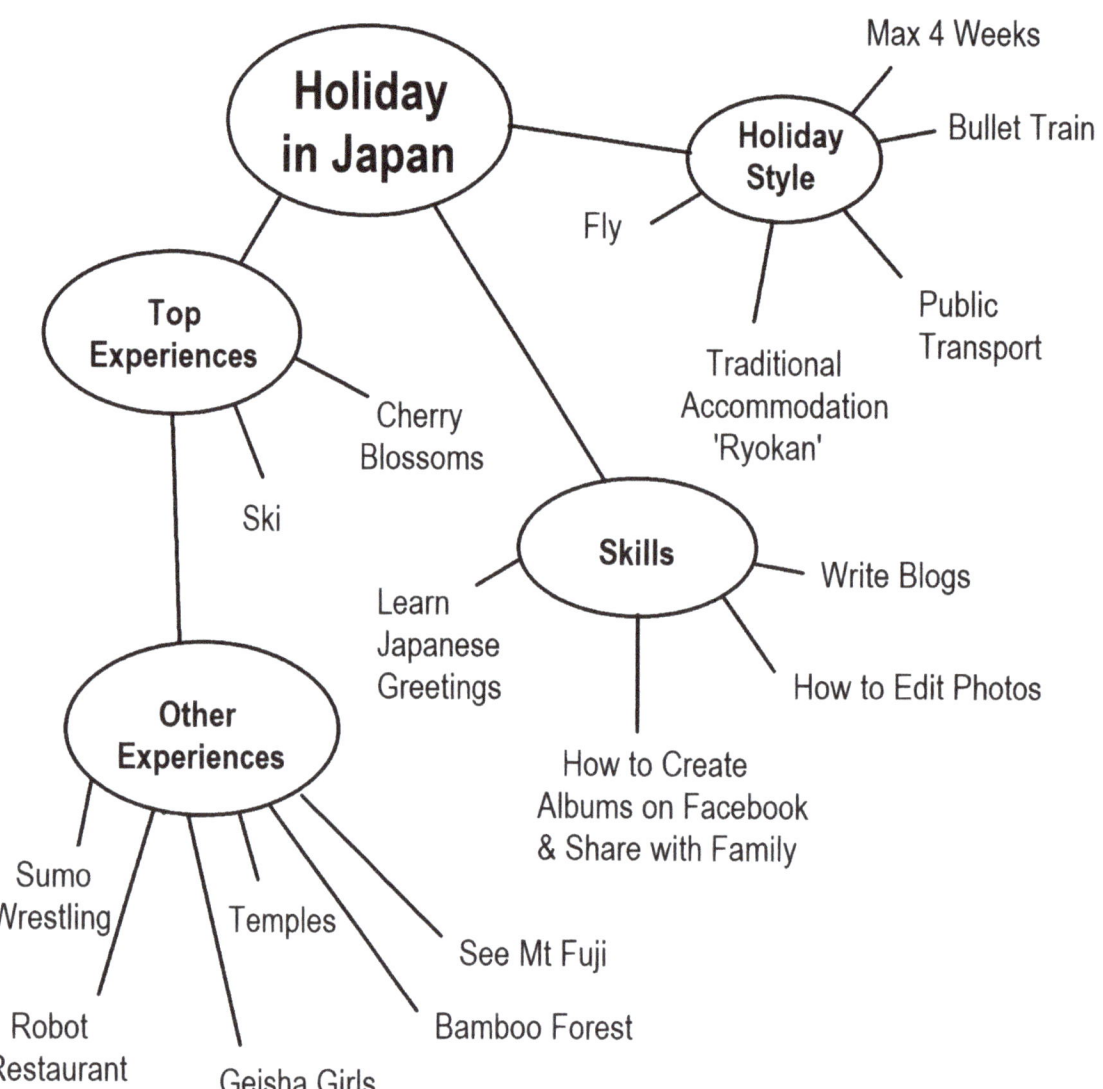

Connecting My Dreams

Put each of your number one dreams into the following circles to create a mind map like our Japan example on the opposite page. Add all the connections you found. Your mind maps will get very messy as you add more and more. Try not to restrict yourself to create the perfect mind map straight away. Simply capture all the connecting ideas.

As you collate all the matching ideas, look
for other things that may stand out.

E.g. To ski in Japan, you need to go in winter. For Cherry Blossoms you go in spring.

Japan Example Continued:

Key Discoveries:

- Skiing is Dec to end March.
- Cherry Blossoms are end March to mid-April and may only last a few days.

Must have:

- Current Passport with more than 6 months from return date of trip
- Approx. four weeks to see everything I plan to see
- Hire Ski Equipment
- Accommodation booked prior to departure

To investigate:

- Best ski fields that suit beginners that are near Kyoto
- When and where can I see Geisha Girls and Sumo wrestling?
- What would I have to book prior to going?
- What won't I need to book?
- How will I get around while in Japan?
- Travel Insurance

My Perfect Home

Key Discoveries:

....

....

....

....

....

Must have:

....

....

....

....

....

Look into:

....

....

....

....

....

Skills to Learn

Key Discoveries:

Must have:

Look into:

Create Awesome
Experiences

Key Discoveries:

Must have:

Look into:

Places to Visit

Key Discoveries:

Must have:

Look into:

Key Discoveries:

Must have:

Look into:

Things to Own

Key Discoveries:

Must have:

Look into:

Key Discoveries:

Must have:

Look into:

Journal Time

THOUGHTS

Write or draw your thoughts

LET'S GET CREATIVE

Creating a visual of your dreams is powerful as it gives you further clarity on what you want, and it helps you FEEL connected to your dream.

The law of attraction is always working on the strongest feelings you have at any one time, so when you create your vision pages with love, excitement and anticipation, then those wonderful feelings flow onto your page. However, if you create your vision page with the thoughts of doubt, that you don't believe it will happen, then that is the feeling that goes into it. Believe in the magic of your dreams and let that energy flow through you.

It is time to play, so have lots of fun and include images of anything and everything that represents your dreams – Brochures, maps, photos, words, colours, magazines.

Create the vision of your dream

On the next couple of pages are some words and statements you may wish to add to your visual pages along with the images you choose.

It can also be very powerful if you include an image of yourself. That way you are putting yourself 'in the picture,' and therefore into the dream.

ORANGE Words

Circle the words that you resonate most with

Dream BIG	Goals	Lifestyle	Fun
Entertainment	Hobbies	Cars	Boats
Holidays	Exotic	5-Star	Destinations
Cruise	Stage	Energy	Action
Independence	Luxury	Ambition	Emotion
Joy	Encouragement	Inspiration	Excitement
Warmth	Service	Laughter	Happiness
Extravagance	Determination	Celebration	Enthusiasm
Expansion	Fascination	Assurance	Earth
Music	Adventure	Environment	Moonlight
Paradise	Tropical	Travel	Mansion
Desire	Confidence	Communication	Style
Adventure	Change	Generosity	Flexibility
Time	Toys	Sunrise	Sunset
Humour	Creativity	Society	Success
Smile	Explore	Imagine	Wisdom

ORANGE Thoughts

Create statements that feel right for you

Clarity on my happiness helps me stay on track	Clarity is Power.
What action can I do right NOW to embrace my Bliss?	Our excuses stop us doing what we really want
My life is getting better & better everyday	Expect Miracles
Dreams come through with the act of 'doing'	I can do it!
Our creative projects bring awareness to the present moment	I am free to be me
Our deepest fear is not that we will fail, it is that we will succeed beyond my wildest dreams	It's cool to be me
When we limit our expectations, we limit our dream	I am true to myself
What action can I do right NOW to embrace my Bliss?	Clarity is Power
We go where our attention goes	My life is magical
I dream big and live big dreams	I choose to be me
Feel the fear and do it anyway	I get what I focus on
Our excuses stop us doing what we really want	I am vibrational energy
I am 100% committed to my happiness	I trust myself
Life is a journey not a destination, I am here to enjoy each moment	I am grateful
The Universe supports my success	I follow my heart

My Perfect Home

Skills to Learn

Create Awesome Experiences

Places to Visit

My Favourite Style of Holiday

Things to Own

Something Else

THOUGHTS

Write or draw your thoughts

BRING IT ALL TOGETHER

Now that you have a reasonably good idea on your top dreams, let's take it one step further. On the next pages you will create a story for your number one dream in each category. Rename the pages to inspiring titles that reflect each dream.

Write your story for each category as if you are living it now. What does it look like? What does it feel like? Who is with you? What are you doing? Imagine each step as you go. Let the dream unfold in as much detail as possible. Imagine it in all its glory.

I believe in my dreams

Remember, happiness is in every step along the way, not just in the end result. It is from the very first inspiration you have, and it stays with you throughout the entire journey. Capture that happiness in your writing. Use descriptive and emotional words to set the scene. Place yourself into each of your dreams.

It is not important to work out all the details on how these dreams will happen for you. Simply imagine it as if it is happening right now.

Once you have your dream stories, then it is time to write your magic story, revise your chaser statements and then rewrite your magic. Although this may feel like you are doubling up, these steps will give you even more clarity and move you closer still to the dreams you are wanting to manifest into your life.

THOUGHTS

Write or draw your thoughts

Manifesting Exercise

A nice little exercise to do prior to writing your stories.

- Find a nice quiet spot, somewhere you feel safe & happy and will not be disturbed.

- Get comfortable sitting or lying

- Take 3 deep breathes in through the nose, out the mouth

- Let your mind wonder all over one of your dreams and see it from all angles, ask to have it in your life.

- Imagine you now have it. See what it looks like. Feel the experience. Acknowledge how you now act and speak.

- Smile and let it flow through your body as if it is real now

- Give thanks to the universe for sending it to you

- Open yourself and accept (or pretend) that it is real now

- You are ready to start writing your story.

Every day upon waking and going to sleep, imagine & feel inspired by one of your dreams as if it is happening now. Your mind will start to open and show you ways for it to come to you. Trust in the process.

My Perfect Home

What is your new title? ....

Are you buying, building, renovating or redecorating your home?

What does the front look like as you drive up? What colour is it? What is the front yard look like? What style of front door do you have? How inviting does it feel?

How many rooms are in the house? What do you use each room for? What colour is it? What is the outlook from each window? How does it make you feel?

Where is it? What is the town like, the street, the neighbours?

Write your story as if you are driving up to your home and then describe each area, how it looks, how it feels and what you do in each one. Describe the outside appearance, how the front and back area look and how you use them. Describe what you love about the area and why you love living there.

E.g. I love the sound of the gravel driveway as I pull up to my beautiful timber home that is nestled in the tropical rainforest. Every time I walk up my front steps, I get such pleasure looking at the handmade leadlight window that I had especially made for my front door. As I am admiring it, I hear the wind chimes playing my favourite sound, welcoming me home...

TITLE:

Skills to Learn

What is your new title? ....

Write as if you have practiced your heart out and now feel confident in it.
What are the details of the skill you have just learnt?
How do you feel now that you have learnt it?
Why did you learn it?
What will it do for you now?
Is this a hobby or a new career path?
Where are you?
Who are you with?
Does it have sound, taste, or colour?

Write your story as if you are now skilled and then use descriptive and emotional words to describe how it looks, how it feels and what you do. Describe what you love about it most and why you are so pleased you chose to learn this skill.

E.g. say you want to learn to paint. What medium are you using? What size is your image? What colours are you using? How it inspires you? What groups do you belong to online and off-line? What videos do you watch? How much time do you spend each day painting? What is your routine now that you are a painter?

I love how I can now paint beautiful pictures that make me feel incredibly connected with myself. I am so proud of myself for making the time and putting in the effort to practice each day. At first I found it a challenge to stay with my routine, and I found it rather intimidating looking at other peoples paintings and then looking at mine. Once I got past criticising my efforts and instead started to praise what I had accomplished, I felt an amazing shift in my skill. I now...

TITLE:

Create Awesome Experiences

What is your new title? ....

Imagine you have just completed your number one experience.

What did you do?
Why did you want to do it?
How did it feel as you were experiencing it?
How do you feel now?
Who was with you?
Did it have sound, taste, or colour?

Write your story as if you have just experienced your number one experience and how awesome you feel right now. Write about how much fun you had leading up to the experience. What were your thoughts? Were you nervous? How did you get over that? Was it as amazing as you had envisaged?

Use descriptive and emotional words to describe what you did, how it looked and felt. Tell the story and describe what you loved about it most and why you are so pleased you chose this experience.

E.g. Say you want to skydive over the Whitsundays. Why did you want to do this? How did you feel? Who is with you? How high was the jump? Were you scared before the jump? What about once you jumped, how did you feel then? Now that you are on the ground and landed safely, how do you feel? Would you do it again?

I have always been afraid of heights, so the idea of skydiving was never on my bucket list until I turned 50. I had always said I want to live till I am 100, so on my 50th birthday I said to myself, 'Girl, if you are going to live till you are 100, then you are just about to start the second half of your life. It's time to get over your fears and start embracing them instead.' That was when I decided it was time to Skydive. As I was getting fitted out and receiving my instructions I felt …

TITLE: ....

....

....

....

....

....

....

....

....

....

....

....

....

....

....

....

....

....

....

....

Places to Visit

What is your new title? ....

Imagine you are now visiting your number one destination.

Where are you?
Who is with you?
What are you doing?
Why did you want to do this?
How do you feel right now?
How did you get there?
Where are you staying? What does that look and feel like?
What sounds do you hear, what colours do you see?

Tell your story as if you are experiencing your number one experience right now. How incredible do you feel right now? Write about how much fun you had getting to this moment. Is it everything you hoped it would be? If it is a travel destination, then get brochures, or go online and read up about it. Add the beautiful descriptions to your story. Use descriptive and emotional words to describe what you did, how it looked and felt. Describe what you love about it most and why you are so pleased you chose this destination.

E.g. Say your number one place to visit was Japan. How do you feel now that you are there? What do you think of the different culture? How are you enjoying the new experiences? The food, the temples, the people. Who is with you? Where are you staying? Why have you chosen this place to visit and the place you are staying? What are all the attractions you are going to? What are the sounds you are experiencing around you? How long are you there for?

I am still pinching myself that I am here! I always thought Japan would be beautiful and knew it had some amazing places to explore, but as I stand here in the bamboo forest, watching two beautiful Geisha girls stroll along, I feel like I am in another world. I ...

94

TITLE:

My Favourite Style of Holiday

What is your new title? ....

How do you love to travel?
What style of transport do you use?
What style of accommodation do you prefer?
What are the main things you look for in this style of holiday?
How long do you like to be away?
What type of destinations do you prefer?
Who is with you?
What do you like about this style of holiday?
Why does it suit you?

Tell your story as if you are currently on one of your favourite styles of holiday. How did you get there? How long are you there for? What are you doing and who are you with? You may have incorporated this with your dream place to visit, or you may have a different dream to write about. Use descriptive and emotional words to describe what you are doing, along with how it looks and feels. Describe what excites you the most and why you choose this style of holiday.

E.g. Say your number one style of holiday is being on a cruise ship. Where are you going on this trip? How long for? What is your cabin like? Do you have a window or a balcony? What places are you visiting? What is the layout of the ship like? What is the food like? How are the wait staff treating you? What other activities are you doing while you are at sea? Who are you with?

Cruising is definitely my kind of holiday and I am loving this trip because ...

98

TITLE:

Things to Own

What is your new title? ....

What is it?
Is it one thing or many?
Why do you want it?
What does it do for you?
How does it make you feel?
How long did it take for you to acquire it?
Is it part of something else?
Is anyone with you?

Tell your story as if you have just acquired that number one thing on your list. How do you feel right now? Use descriptive and emotional words to describe it in detail, how it looks and how it feels. Describe what excites you the most and why.

E.g. Say your number one thing you want is a convertible and you have just purchased it. What make and model is it? What features does it have? What colour is it? Who is with you when you buy it?

I love my convertible. I was extremely lucky to find this one and it is everything I desired and more. I feel so free driving along the freeway with the roof down and the wind blowing in my hair. I am very happy because...

TITLE:

Something Else

What is your new title? ....

What it is?
How does it make you feel?
Does it have a colour, smell, taste, texture or sound?
Who is with you?
How long did it take you to get/do it?
Why is it so important to you?

Tell your story as if you have whatever it is that is on your list for this category. Describe it as if it is real right now? Use descriptive and emotional words to describe what you are doing, along with how it looks and feels. Describe what excites you the most and why you chose this.

E.g. Say you have a dream to write a book. You may have listed a number of skills to learn and experiences to have in earlier categories, and here you want to explore the dream of how it will feel once you have published the book. Is it fiction or non-fiction? What is it about? Why did you feel called to write it? Describe the book. What does it look like? Who is reading it? How do they feel once they have read it? Who published it? What does your life look like now that you are a published author?

I always thought I would write a book, although I had no idea how that would happen, and yet here I am, a published author. I felt so inspired to write because …

TITLE:

THOUGHTS

Write or draw your thoughts

It's Magic

You have a magical wand and you have three wishes. You can choose three of your favourite dreams and create a fairy-tale story, an imaginary story where you have all three wishes now.

Where are you? What does it look like? What does it feel like? Who is with you? What are you doing? Describe the excitement that you feel as you are living your three dreams.

Before writing, take time to be still and go within. Feel yourself full of gratitude for all the wonderful things you already have, then ask your inner child to help select three wishes so you can write your fairy-tale.

Wishes

1) ....

2) ....

3) ....

....

....

....

....

....

....

Life is magical when I live in the high energy vibrations of love and gratitude

Revising my Chaser Thoughts

Go back to your Chaser page and have a good look at what you have captured. These are the thoughts that stop us doing what we want in life. They come from your belief system and outside influences from when you were very young. None of them are true, although they seem true when you hear them because they are familiar to you.

A thought from your heart, from your inner self, is always loving and supportive, NEVER negative. A thought from your mind is usually judgmental, criticising or disempowering in some way. It is simply how the sub-conscious mind gets programmed.

To understand this better, download the *Rainbow Vision Journal free eBook.*

Look at each chaser thought and see if there are any recurring patterns or themes. Then take each thought and create an empowering statement from it. E.g. I can't do this, can become, I am able to achieve what my heart desires.

Old thought ....

....

New empowering thought ....

....

Old thought ....

....

New empowering thought ....

....

Old thought

New empowering thought

Old thought

New empowering thought

Old thought

New empowering thought

Old thought

New empowering thought

Old thought

New empowering thought

Old thought

New empowering thought

Old thought

New empowering thought

Old thought

New empowering thought

THOUGHTS

Write or draw your thoughts

The Magic Rewritten

Now that you have revised your chaser thoughts and seen what is holding you back, go back and relook at your magical story with your three wishes.

Rewrite your magical story using your new empowering statements. Make your magical story powerful by weaving your new affirmations through it. You have the wand. You have the ability to create your life however you choose. So, what do you choose now? Ask yourself if it feels right for you. This is the most important question. The better it makes you feel, the more it is your true alignment so embrace it. Do not think about how your magical story will happen, only what it is like once you are there.

Believe in the magic of your story and trust that once you are clear on what you really what, it will come to you in ways you would never expect.

Before you rewrite your story, stop and ask for guidance. What is your heart telling you?

E.g. where you may have written 'I wish' or 'I want,' change your words to 'I have' or 'I enjoy.' Remember you can say what you want, so long as it is uplifting – you have the magic wand!

3 Action Steps

Look at your top dream statements and your magical story. What 3 actions can you do right now to start bringing your number one goals into fruition? Insert each step into your calendar and set reminders to stay focused. Remember all new skills take practice.

This is my commitment to myself and my happiness

I wear ORANGE to remind myself of my Path

THOUGHTS

Write or draw your thoughts

My Reward

How will you reward yourself once you have completed all three steps?

Make your reward something that you would not normally do for yourself so that when you have completed your three steps, you feel excited and enjoy your reward. Then use your excitement to create another three steps and keep your momentum going.

What will happen if I don't Complete my steps? How will I feel?

Write or draw your thoughts

Check In

How do you feel now that you are more aware of all the dreams that lie in your heart? Do you feel happier now than when you started your journal? Remember life is a journey. You are not rushing to be somewhere, you are on a journey to do, be and have, the best life you can experience. This is your purpose for your whole life, to enjoy as many moments as you can. To be happy and to be the best version of yourself that you can be. The more you choose to be true to yourself, the more life gives you the experiences that make your heart sing. No one has the power to make you happy, except you. Choose to be happy by choosing to live from your heart.

Take some time to reflect through everything you have written. Add to it wherever it feels right. You can redo this journal every year as a refresher on what is important to you at that time. Things change and so might your dreams as you become more aware of who you truly are.

The steps you have learnt in this journal can be applied to everything in your life, not just your big dreams. It is the same process. Decide what is important and why. Get clear on how it feels, imagine it is real for you right now and write out that story. Believe in your dream, be thankful for it, feel the happiness of it flow through you and allow it to come to you however it unfolds and allow yourself to enjoy the journey.

It really is all up to you

You can have a lovely magical life, it's not hard, it just takes a bit of effort and commitment on your behalf. The great thing is, you can think about most of these things wherever you are. If you are standing in a queue, stuck in traffic, or simply washing your hair; you can raise your energy vibration by thinking about your dreams. You can choose to daydream about your wonderful life as if it is already true for you, or you can choose instead to dwell on how it is not yet a part of your life. The first thought will help bring dreams to you, while the second thought will help push them away. It is your choice.

Enjoy your dreams and continue your drawing and writing practice on the next pages.

Journal Time – Keep up the Magic

If You Can Dream It, You Can Do It

What's Next?

The ORANGE Vision was the second part of a series of seven steps in following your heart to your pot of GOLD.

The next step is YELLOW – My Well-Being.

**How to feel good regardless of
Your body shape or fitness level**

YELLOW is where we start to learn how to listen to our
body and take notice of what it is telling us.

To learn more about YELLOW, visit
www.rainbowvisionjournal.com/yellow

Continue journaling to gain clarity on your true self.
Practicing every day to draw like a child and write from within

It really is the easiest way to learn how to follow your heart

DRAW LIKE A CHILD

DRAW LIKE A CHILD

DRAW LIKE A CHILD

DRAW LIKE A CHILD

DRAW LIKE A CHILD

DRAW LIKE A CHILD

DRAW LIKE A CHILD

DRAW LIKE A CHILD

DRAW LIKE A CHILD

DRAW LIKE A CHILD

DRAW LIKE A CHILD

You can choose how your life unfolds

Congratulations
on reaching the end of your journal

Well done! Now that you have completed all this in-depth work, don't let it slip away. Set up a daily ritual with the intention of topping up your energy vibration as a constant reminder of all the love, support and dreams you have no matter what is transpiring in your life.

Remember, you have the power to choose your thoughts and your responses; and with each, your energy vibration goes out to the universe and then reflects back to you. When you choose to think and respond from love, you get love. When you choose from fear, you get fear.

Being aware of your thoughts and feelings then choosing to align them with your true heart's desire, is what creates an awesome life. You have the power to do it, you just need to believe in yourself and practice it for just five minutes every day. When you choose to make it a way of life that you cherish, it will become your life, and that is when the magic really happens.

Don't forget your free gifts on page ix

To receive further support on your journey into awareness, go to
www.rainbowvisionjournal.com

The YELLOW journal is next in this series and is about your well-being. It is where you will become aware of what your body is telling you so that you can feel better within yourself. The journal builds on the things you love from RED, and the dreams you have in ORANGE and helps you work out how to look after yourself without worrying about fad diets or gym memberships.

It is learning to listen to your body
And your inner child

Stay true to yourself

NAMASTE

(I bow to the divine in you)

Lightning Source UK Ltd.
Milton Keynes UK
UKHW051318200820
368534UK00003B/28